MW00935794

Advertising, Branding & Marketing 101

The Small Business Owner's Guide to Making Branding, Marketing, and Advertising Much More Effective

By Dixie Maria Carlton

Published by: Maria Carlton Pty Ltd
                  www.AuthorityAuthors.com.au
                  QLD 4019, Australia
ISBN: 978-1545474082

For Nix and Alex

CONTENTS

Foreword

Your brand is not your logo, and your advertising is not your marketing. These are two common misconceptions that can make 'marketing' seem quite complicated. In just about any industry, not understanding the jargon can trip up newcomers. But when it comes to marketing your understanding of the basics can potentially save you thousands of dollars on advertising, marketing and branding.

- Identifying Your Target Markets
- Marketing and Brand Planning
- Media and Promotions
- Websites
- Customer Service
- Gaining Repeat and New Business
- Building Your Reputation Through Public Relations

This book will help you to understand the basics of business and marketing plans, branding, image, customer service and public relations so that you can grow your business through simple and smart marketing practices. Getting the basics right can make such a difference to the outcomes. Measuring the results of your advertising can lead to effective decision making about what to spend and where to invest your marketing budget.

Many marketing professionals and business advisors use terms like business plan, marketing plan, branding, image, customer service, public relations, advertising and logos – and yet their clients often don't understand them well.

When you understand 'how it works' you get a lot more punch out of your advertising and marketing campaigns. You will also have more realistic expectations of the results you can expect from your marketing and will be able to work more effectively with your advisors.

I've filled this book with explanations, ideas and inspiration to help you tackle this critical area of your business and plan growth and increased profitability through smart (and that does not mean expensive) marketing, designed to turn your clients into raving fans. Raving fans are the kind of customers who keep coming back to your business and keep sending their friends to you.

Dixie Maria Carlton

1

Understanding the Basics

When putting together a business plan, most people start with a list of who they are, where they're located and what they do. These are the 'who, what and where I am' facts of being in business. However, as important as these areas are, when you create a marketing plan, you need to turn these 'I AM' points into 'FOR YOU' points that will interest your customers and prospects.

Do this by tackling the WHO, WHAT, WHERE, WHEN and HOW of marketing basics. Putting a marketing plan together is not only vital to good business planning but by separating the marketing/media plan from the business/cash flow plan, it's a lot easier to update and review regularly.

Business Plan vs Marketing Plan – What is the difference?

A *business* plan is essentially a list of all the information you need to identify about your business for the benefit of your partners, shareholders, bankers and accountant. It contains information such as what your product or service is, the market you are supplying to, what your expected turnover is, and what your own and your competitors' strengths and weaknesses are.

A *marketing* plan is more focused on how you propose to grow your business and where you will commit your advertising and marketing resources to achieve the outcomes suggested in your business plan. A marketing plan identifies your customers, how to reach them, how to treat them, and your strategy for encouraging referral and repeat business. It is also where you discuss your brand plan, and how you will create and then promote your brand as part of your marketing plan.

Many business owners write a comprehensive business plan when they start their business and find the process so arduous that they never review it again. This is usually one document that combines business, marketing, media, and cash flow planning, but this can be made a lot simpler if you separate them. A business plan may not need to be updated quite as often as much of the information contained within just this part will remain the same from year to year. I recommend reviewing the strengths, weaknesses and opportunities in your market every year as part of your planning, but don't feel you have to completely re-write the business plan document more often than perhaps every 2 – 4 years.

However, your marketing plan must be reviewed *every* year, along with the media plan – the part of the document that outlines where and how often you will use promotional advertising, branding, public relations and merchandising tools for enhancing and growing your business and brand(s).

There is a trend for business plans to be updated and reviewed every quarter. For some types of businesses and for some managers who are confident of working in this way, that can be a great option. But it's not for everyone, and getting the basic part of business and marketing planning working for you is your primary goal. Time frames for this may change when you feel ready to do that if it suits your company.

Business Plan

Your business plan does not have to be a 100-page novella, and keeping it very simple will make regular updating easy. Annually or at least biennial updates are highly recommended by most business consultants in this fast changing economic and technology-based business world.

Getting started can be as easy as starting with a list of bullet points for each question and answering them one by one. Keep your answers brief (just one or two sentences); anything longer is better left for a company profile.

The Main Points or Questions:
- What is Your Business?

- In the simplest terms – what do you do? Keep it short, and explain it as you would to your children.

For example:

"We are product manufacturers specializing in plastic molded Safety Widgets".

Your purpose and your mission statement will be closely linked, but you may express it one way for public consumption (i.e. in your mission statement), and in another way in your own business plan.

What is Your Mission Statement?

Why are you here – what is your business purpose? Again, this does not have to need not be long and complicated. For example, *"We are here to provide a new style of service in the sales and production of Safety Widgets".*

You could go further and say: *"Our revolutionary style of installation and sales of Safety Widgets for home owners is designed to ensure increased safety in every household in Australia. We will create a radically new way of thinking about safety measures in homes across the country."*

What is Your Vision?

Your vision statement is the promise you may give to your clients and employees outlining what you want to achieve with your business over a period of time. It could read something like this:

"We will partner our clients – distributors and agents - to assist in penetrating 75% of Australian homes within the next 24 months. Within five years we will have 95% of homes installed with our brand of Safety Widget.

Additional products are being developed to complement sales of this key item and will be ready for release into our (by then) existing market in three years' time."

S.W.O.T. Analysis

A basic element of every good business plan should include an S.W.O.T. analysis – a dissection of your Strengths, Weaknesses, Opportunities, and Threats. I recommend paying particular attention to your opportunities and threats as these are the areas which will challenge your creativity the most, but will also help to reveal your best areas for potential growth. For example, if you are threatened by regular price cutting from your main competitor, then this is an area your S.W.O.T. analysis to identify. You will then be able to work on a strategy for surmounting this problem and you may even help create an opportunity for turning this to your advantage.

What are Your Strengths?

There are likely to be particular areas where you know you are better than just about everyone else and can state that proudly and confidently.

The strengths section of your business plan is where you need to think about why your business has the edge over your competitors and how you can focus on further developing and protecting these areas.

For example, it's worth promoting the fact that you have the most advanced technology – and it may generate the best returns overall – but bear in mind that maintaining that edge could be expensive.

Some other examples of strengths might include:

- *"Our comprehensive research shows that we are the only producers of this product in the South Pacific. Other competitors' products are more expensive to market because they are imported from Europe."*

- *"We have world-recognized experts on our team."*

- *"We are quick to market place because we produce and market the product. And, for the same reason, we reduce time delays between production, distribution and marketing".*

What are Your Weaknesses?

Every company has areas that can benefit from operational improvements and they may change from time to time. Sometimes your greatest strengths can also be your greatest weakness. For example, if one of your key people is someone that your customers particularly like to work with, then using him or her as the figurehead can be a great way to promote your services. However, if that person does not delegate well and leaves a big gap if unavailable due to holiday or illness, then the company's greatest strength becomes its greatest weakness.

Some other examples of areas where a company may identify areas of weakness include:

- *"We are under-capitalized by up to 30% of our preferred start position."*

- *"Our competitors are prepared to undercut our prices in order to retain their market share – even if that means selling below profitability."*

- *"Our sales team needs to be trained extremely well to sell this product – but it is not a standard and easy-to-understand product."*

Once you know your weak areas, it's very important to identify ways to overcome them in the long and short term.

What are Your Opportunities?

There may be various things happening around your industry, town or country that can provide big opportunities for you to tap into. Maybe a tender is coming up, or a first-to-market opportunity for one of your services or products. Perhaps your product or service is affected by surges in tourism.

Here you could list points like:

"We have identified a potential large market for our Safety Widgets in Asia, which is currently not being supplied at all."

"We have the best product on the market and, given the right information, people will buy our product over the competitors, basing their decision on quality and not just than price."

What are the Potential Threats to Your Success?

Potential threats can come at you from any direction.

Perhaps you worry that a major competitor may one day launch a product that will bowl yours over. Or a problem might arise from within. What if one of your key players falls ill or gets pregnant? What if it's you with a health challenge? Dealing with something like that can take a lot to resolve.

List your possible 'Oh my God, what if THIS happens...' things, and take steps (including taking out income protection or partnership insurance) to help give you necessary peace of mind.

Other 'Success-threats' may include:

- *"Another company has commenced research into our type of product."*

- *"We have not been able to secure our production manager by having him sign a confidentiality agreement with a restraint-of-trade clause."*

- *"Other businesses like ours, that may become competitors, are aware of our presence and structure."*

What are Your Human Resource Needs?

One of the reasons you may be in business is to grow it and earn more money. An upside of taking time to develop your business and marketing plan is to prepare for that growth, which often means an increase in staff.

For example, you may write something like:

- *"Today we have three sales people, six production crew and two managers – one of whom is a marketing person."*

- *"In 12 months, we anticipate needing five sales people, eight production people and an assistant marketing manager."*

Another HR need may be for increased training, or for specialized skills obtainable only through the use of contractors or consultants.

For example:

"As we prepare our new division we will need to engage technical specialists to assist in installing the required software and hardware we will be purchasing. This investment in human capital will be short term, and we will then employ a graduate for ongoing and permanent support of this technology".

What About Money?

What are your short to medium-term growth plans in relation to your financial position?

Let's continue to use the Safety Widgets as an example:

- *"We need to operate on the basis of 100 potential sales in the first three months, at turnover of $xxx, increasing to an average of 200 sales per month for the following six months once our marketing has started to have an impact and our sales people have become familiar with the product and the sales system."*

- *"We require only 50 sales per month to cover our costs."*

Strategic Alliances

Can you identify any potential strategic alliances with like-minded companies who can help you fast track your success by joint marketing, export or any other means? In the building trade, a common strategic alliance might be formed between various trades-people, such as builder and architect, or mortgage broker and real estate agent. In the fashion trade, a retailer might team up with a beauty therapist or hair salon for joint promotions. The idea would be to share the cost of targeting the same market and then share the resulting benefits. Strategic alliances must be win/win partnerships and reviewed regularly so as to maximize the relationship and the benefits each party derives from it.

Strategic Milestones
How will you know when you are achieving your plans? Set in place some future progress points that will assure you of forward movement. These may include reaching and maintaining a specific monthly turnover, or hiring another staff member.

Identify and write down what you wish to achieve within definite time frames and check them off as you reach them.

Cash Flow Forecast
Your cash flow forecast will identify exactly what this financial growth and profitability picture looks like – so there is no need to go into detailed explanations about your early growth and financial situation in this part of your plan.

A cash flow plan does need to identify your fixed costs, variable costs, and projected turnover. Is there likely to be a potential up-turn or down-turn due to seasonal variations? This also needs to be accommodated in your planning.

Fixed costs may include rent, loan payments, insurance, power, phones and salaries. Variable costs may include purchases, stationery, wages and commissions, training, travel, entertainment, bank fees, accountant and legal fees, subscriptions and anything else that may vary from month to month. Some things may be more relative to 'cost of sales'. For example freight may be a cost that is directly related to how many units are sold. These could also just as easily be a cost of prospecting for new business, in which case they will be classed as just another variable cost.

In determining what is fixed and what is variable, decide what costs are going to remain firm regardless of how many employees you have, how many items you sell and how much control you have over the amounts each month.

Circumstances may change through the year. Knowing what you hope to achieve and having a clear picture of the *expected* outcomes, makes it easier to work out a plan that can take any changes into account. Therefore, work out where you can *expect* to be sitting financially in six months, 12 months and even two years from now assuming all variables have been allowed for in your plan to the best of your ability, but allow for the fact that it may also feel a lot like crystal ball gazing.

As you can see, a business plan can be very simple and only a couple of pages long. This makes an annual update quite straightforward. On the other hand, a marketing plan is a little more complex, but tells the story of how your company will move forward. This should be updated every one or two years, complete with a media plan that explains how your advertising dollars will be spent.

Think of it as a map for reaching your expected or required growth.

2

Targeting Your Market

First you have to understand who you are, and

who your customers are.

WHO Do You Serve?

You have certain products or services and your mission is to sell as many of these as possible. To do this easily, you will need to know exactly who makes the decisions about purchasing your product of service. Your business may serve certain ages, genders, groups and families, and their wants or needs. It's important to clearly identify exactly who you are marketing to. Can you identify the *psychographic* and *demographic* profile of your ideal client? For example, is it male or female, domestic or industrial, old or young, conservative or radical, internal or external? Do you sell business-to-business or to a consumer market?

Let's work with our safety widgets product again and consider a full psycho/demo-graphic of this customer:

Profiling Your Customers

This information helps to identify how you can best reach your ideal customers through a range of media and marketing opportunities. This is critical information, as it helps to narrow down the range of available options for your advertising dollars. A *psychographic* profile tells you about someone's lifestyle.

For example:

"Our typical client listens to XYZ radio stations; watches ABC TV shows, reads women's magazines and Readers' Digest. She takes holidays with her family once a year to an overseas or local destination, and spends approximately $2000 - $5000 per year on herself with beauty treatments and fashion items. She lives in the suburbs, with a nice garden and spends time on her own and her children's additional sports and club activities."

A *demographic* profile reveals age, marital and family status, and income.

For example:

"Mainly women, aged 20–40, mothers of young and mainly pre-teenage children with a household income of $60-$120k"

If you think you are selling a product to people who are *all households, all ages* – in short, ***all people*** – then you are fooling yourself. For example, I recently met a supplier of household security alarms and monitoring products. I asked him who his main market was and he said *everyone* was his market. He told me that he sold to large homes, small homes, university students, elderly people and his advertising reached everyone. Initially he could not see that his most easily reached target market was 'me'. When we worked out my age, lifestyle, home location and income level we found I was right in the middle of his targeted demographic but was completely overlooked in his advertising and marketing planning. In fact, as we delved deeper into his business, we discovered that most of his business was really with families in their 30s and 40s, not young people renting or elderly people.

In merely scattering some ads in the university newspaper, and the local free paper and having his vehicle and business premises sign-written, he had failed to focus on reaching middle-upper income level home owners in a reasonably affluent area, who were not only security conscious, but had the funds to spend on his middle-high end products and monitoring services.

These people were also aged between 35 and 55 with parents aged 60-80 who would be easily targeted as good prospects for medical and security alarm monitoring. In addition, they had a high number of children in the 17 – 25 age range. If this man considered developing his database he could easily find an eager target market for his special student and rental car alarm systems.

Knowing who your target market is helps to identify ways to best target them and use your marketing dollars most cost effectively.

WHAT is Your Product or Service?

Do you have an easy, succinct way of describing your skills so that others can quickly understand what you can do for them? If, for example, the only thing you say on meeting a potential new customer is that you *'work in insurance'* or *'sell safety widgets'* or are *'a builder'*, how interested are they likely to be in wanting to know more?

What you need is an audio logo.

Develop an Audio Logo and a Half Minute Advertisement

Whenever you meet people you get only a very short opportunity to impress them, and new conversation often turns to asking, *'what do you do?'* Here is where you turn, *'I work in insurance'* into, *'I help people take risks and still sleep well'*, or *'I sell Safety Widgets'* can become into *'I keep people safe in their homes every day'*.

You could also turn, *'I am a builder'* into, *'I build beautiful homes for people who can afford something a little different but don't want to spend 50 years paying for it'.*

Any kind of basic 'I do this' can be altered into something that will inspire a new contact to ask for more information.

In a busy room you may only get a moment or two say something so compelling that your target feels he or she must ask for your card or seek you out later.

If there's more time to expand on your audio logo then and there, make sure you have a well-rehearsed 30-second (approximately) speech that explains your business in more detail.

It may sound something like this:

Expand, *"I help people to take risks and still sleep well"* to, *"This means that I help people to work out tailor-made living assurance and financial planning needs. My specialty is ensuring that if you become ill or suffer an accident that keeps you down for six months to six years, your lifestyle and family commitments are still covered."*

Or – *"I help to ensure that if there's a general safety failure of electrical work in homes, an alarm is triggered to give people enough time to resolve the problem before disaster strikes".*

Or – *"I have developed a special system of construction for larger homes that makes them much more affordable for families who might normally only be able to afford very small homes".*

Well-rehearsed lines like these ensure that new contacts will want to know more. You will also stick in their memories in part because you have turned a possibly ordinary service or product into something which sounds vitally interesting and partly because you did not falter and stumble over your explanation in the way so many of us do.

The words you say should simply explain what dilemma or challenge you could solve for them (even those ones they don't yet know they have). If you can explain, 'this is what can we do *for you*' instead of just *'this is what we do'*, it makes people far more likely to think about how you could help them with needs they may not even have considered before.

If your company has several solutions for your prospects and clients, then use this strategy for each solution. For instance, the security business owner mentioned earlier would need three separate audio logos or quick speeches – one for middle-income residents needing home security, one for students or flatters wanting a portable system, and a different approach again for seniors needing a medical alarm.

More on Audio Logos

For best success with your audio logo, deliver it with confidence and then quickly-turn the conversation over to your new contact. Ask questions, find out what they do and how they might become customers. After all, everyone loves to talk about themselves and if they have a problem you can help with then it's very useful to find out a little more about them before you get to the point of giving your card. When you suggest a meeting, it means that you will have a much clearer idea of how you will pitch your business solutions to them. Don't just deliver your audio logo and follow up by diving straight in to seeing if you can make this person a new prospect... use it to open them up first.

WHERE Do You and Your Clients Operate From?

Where you operate from and where you work with your clients may not be the same place. Your business premises may be distant from your client making it impractical or burdensome for them to come to you.

You may work from an office at home or a virtual office in your car... in which case, you need to let your prospects know that you will come to see them. Some of my business meetings are better conducted in cafes, as this is a way to meet with clients or customers in a semi-formal setting. Sometimes a conference telephone option or Skype works well too.

Turning this into a 'where we can best serve you?' exercise will involve thinking about what will best suit your customers. If, they need to see samples of your work or a showroom display, how can you make it more worthwhile for them? Perhaps you can add an incentive somehow.

Meet in an environment which suits the type of meeting you are having and in which the comfort level of the client is best accommodated.

WHY Do Your Customers Need You?

Why should your customers work with you instead of your competitors? What makes you so much better than someone else who offers a similar product or service? You need to develop your Unique Selling Proposition.

Decide on What Exactly You do that is:

- Different
- Better
- More specialized
- Sets you apart

Be firm about this as it is what your reputation will be built on. Try writing this down on a piece of paper:

Why Do Your Customers Want You?

Sometimes your customers just simply like you. In fact, some customers will spend money on your business because they like to spend time with you or a particular member of your team. Take for example the lady who lives alone and loves to spend money on beauty crèmes or coffee shops because it gets her into conversations with people behind a counter. Or consider the restaurant or bar for whom some of the regular patrons are there because the food is good, but mostly the bar staff are friendly.

For some customers, their reasons for going somewhere is that the 'vibes' are good, and they like to look at the décor. Business is about relationships, and successful relationship building will result in successful sales being made. When it comes to selling, people will only buy from people they don't like if they absolutely have to – but more people will buy from people they do like, even if the actual purchase may be unnecessary.

Your Unique Selling Proposition

Your USP is best used to help establish that price is not your main competitive advantage. Ideally you want to have your customers deal with you because they like your quality, service or unique features. This enables you to charge a fair but reasonable rate, and helps to guard against any price undercutting by your competitors. In fact, this can make many companies almost untouchable by their rivals, and helps to ensure much stronger loyalty for long-term customer relationships.

For example, a builder who quotes on new homes and is pinning all his hopes on being in at the right price, is in a much more precarious position than the builder who has built a solid reputation for completing excellent quality work on time and on budget, is easy to contact and get along with, and does great after-contract inspections.

Our first example may present a cheaper quote, but many people will think it's worth paying more for quality and peace of mind.

There will always be consumers who buy on price. But if you position your products or services to those who want more than that – and there are just as many who do – then not only will you enjoy a slightly or even significantly better margin, you also end up attracting better quality (more enjoyable to work for) customers.

Work out what your unique selling position is by trying this exercise:

Most companies in our industry do...

My company also does...

List as many unique or extra things you can think of. Then identify which one(s) your customers value most highly and promote it or them.

Establish your Unique Selling Proposition before marketing yourself to potential clients. Your reputation will rest on the DIFFERENCES between you and your competitors.

HOW Do You Do What You Do?

This is part of the 'why' factor – it is what makes you better and opens the way to explain to your customers how some of the things that may be taken for granted in your industry are handled better by your company.

For example, in some building trades you will help your case by stating clearly that your policy is to leave the site spotless when you complete a job. Customer service may be a given for many businesses to offer, but explaining what your actual stance is on this will serve you well.

If you do have a better-than-industry-average way of doing what you do, then getting that fact right out there for your customers and prospects will help form their expectations of your service and make it easier for you to exceed them. *Meeting* a customer's expectations is a good way to hold on to them. *Exceeding* their expectations is a great way to get them telling all their friends about you.

Carefully define what is different about your product or service so that no one is left in any doubt about what it is that you do. It may be that you write these differences into the contract.

Why Are You Doing This?

If you were creating bricks, would it be to make bricks or to contribute to the building of a new hospital?

Disney wants to make people happy; Nike wants to be ahead of the rest. *Why* are you doing what you do?

People generally won't care about what you do until they know you care about them. Understanding your WHY is a very important part of your marketing planning.

3

Positioning Your Business

This is about knowing your purpose, mission or vision and then making sure you have clearly identified these to your customers.

During the early stages of a business relationship there will be many so-called 'moments of truth' when your customers can be turned on or off. Identifying them early makes it easier to address them and make subtle or bigger changes necessary to ensure happy and satisfied customers.

Part of positioning relies on having your customers understand where you fit in their perception of your industry. For example, if you own a restaurant, is it seafood oriented? If so, then do you have a high priced, or low cost menu, plastic table cloths or linen, special signature dishes, a great ambience and meeting place for business people, lovers on a date, or mothers having lunch together while their children are at school? Are you a laid-back casual-dress style of place or do you maintain minimum dress standards?

Positioning is about having an easy way of situating your particular style of restaurant in their minds so that people immediately understand what sort of place you are before they even enter for the first time. The same applies with any kind of business. Let's consider a legal firm in the same way. Do you position yourself as specialist or general practice, expensive, mid-range, or very affordable? Are you big or small, friendly, approachable, savvy and dynamic or practical and down to earth so that everyone understands you and loves you?

Having a clear position helps to ensure that your brand plan is focused on delivering this position in the minds of your potential customers. Everything that you do with regards to your image must reflect that position, from the pens with your logo on, to the dress standards of your employees, and the way your advertising is managed, and what style of promotions you do.

Khan Auschwissimbalmk or Kim Austin?

Your name can be hard or easy to say or spell. Is it an advantage or a disadvantage? If it's the latter then consider changing it for business. Words that are easy to say and write will serve you much better than a name that your staff members have trouble repeating and your customers struggle to recall.

Although creative mileage can sometimes be derived from unusual names, you need an original angle that works and can be sold in a clever way to your customers, for example Renee Zellwegger and Arnold Swartzenegger have used this to their advantage. It may even mean poking a little bit of fun at yourself.

Once you have confirmed your business name, you need to remember that for people to relate it to what you do, you need a positioning statement.

Your Positioning Statement

This is what makes your name stick in people's minds in the place you want to *own* in their minds. If you want them to think of you as the bargain king, the creative genius, the tastiest, classiest, strongest, funniest, warmest or cleanest... then you need to say you are 'THAT', in such a way that they remember you or automatically think of you for being just exactly THAT.

Some Examples:

- Pepsi – *A new generation*
- Burger King – *Flame grilled freshness*
- McDonalds – *I'm loving it!*
- New Zealand – *100% Pure*
- Singapore – *The cleanest city in the world*

- Toyota – *For everyday people*
- Volvo – *The world's safest cars*
- Avis – *We try harder*
- The Warehouse – *Where everyone gets a bargain*
- L'Oreal– *Because you're worth it*

A clear positioning statement helps the customer to get clear in his or her mind what to expect from that particular brand. For example, if you stepped off the plane in New Zealand and only visited downtown or suburban Auckland, you would probably feel cheated by not having seen the lovely green landscapes and forests that New Zealand features in its international tourism ads. Singapore boasts of having the cleanest city in the world, so to see litter on the streets would surprise you, because you *expect* to see it clean – and not just a little less messier than maybe London or Los Angeles.

The Warehouse – 'where everyone gets a bargain', suggests that they have a lot of everything there, and that you should expect to find at least a few things to purchase at a very low price.

L'Oreal tells women that we are all worth whatever it is that they have to offer that will make us feel gorgeous – in four simple words – *"Because you're worth it"*.

A positioning statement needs to be seen or mentioned every time your name is seen or mentioned. It sits there as a supporting tag-line to help make your business memorable.

4

Customer Service Essentials

Never Underestimate the Importance of Having a Great Customer Service Plan

Before, during and after someone has had some contact with you, you owe it to yourself and your long-term success to take control and orchestrate the experience. Don't just open the doors every day and imagine happy customers returning time and again just because you are there, hoping it will happen.

If you want repeat and referral business, then you must plan for it. It's part of your marketing plan and we will divide it into three parts – before, during and after sales customer service.

Before

Decide how people will feel when they walk in your door. Is the reception area comfortable, warm and inviting? Does the person answering your telephone sound cheerful and capable? Can they put callers through to the right person without leaving them hanging on hold for minutes, or worse, accidentally cutting the connection or getting the lines mixed up?

You can extend the 'Before' Customer service to include what happens if they encounter one of your staff in an elevator, or standing in line at the petrol station counter or coffee house. If your staff are identifiable as working for you, (company car, logo on clothing, badge on shirt), then ensuring that they always act courteously can be implemented as company policy, and written into employment contracts if necessary. After all, everyone they meet while they're working could be a current or future customer.

If part of your service is promoted as friendly and helpful, this should not be limited only to set times, places and situations. It should be offered all the time and by all of your team.

During

If you have firm policies about how prospects and customers will be treated *before* they agree to spend money and time with you, then this service must continue, and improvements to enhance the relationship are paramount in any interaction you and your staff have with them over time.

Your marketing strategy and budget may include a gift with purchase or you may decide to offer incentives on follow-up purchases. You might set up loyalty programs or send promotional products to remind the customer that you appreciate their business. For example, a card sent with the simple message *"We trust that all is going well with your recent purchase and please call again soon"*, will be appreciated, and even more so if it is accompanied with a voucher for a value-add service to enjoy on the next visit.

After

Sending a token of your appreciation for prompt payment of accounts and making follow-up phone or visits to your customers will go a long way towards keeping them loyal, while also giving you opportunities to learn how your products or services could be improved.

Of course, you can 'wow' them even as you serve them. It may be as simple as offering to carry the purchases to the car, offering a free trial of a new product, remembering their name (a great one for restaurants) or asking if everything is okay while they are standing waiting or looking around. The way in which you make someone feel welcome, offer refreshments, and then follow through can often make the difference between whether what they tell a friend about you, or forget to talk about you at all.

For example, if you are a service company and you frequently offer people a drink while they are spending time in your waiting room, then going the extra mile and offering *real* coffee, herbal or regular tea, and serving it in very nice cups, will set your waiting-room experience apart from many others.

Offering to walk mum and dad's small child across the floor to the play area while they talk to the sales person will make the sales process feel a lot more relaxed. Relaxed selling is usually a lot more productive and satisfactory for both parties. Great customer service doesn't have to be expensive, just simple and effective, but you still need to make sure that everyone on your team knows your customer-service plan is part of your marketing plan – which is aimed at getting more repeat and referral business.

Your Business Philosophy

This is the list of do's and don'ts you may print out or even display publicly for your staff and customers to see. Some things on it may relate to customer service, and some may be about marketing or price policies.

Whether you make this a public statement or not, at least knowing firmly what your rules are, and ensuring that they are aligned with your values (internal motivators such as honesty, fairness, value, service), can be an additional enhancement to your marketing plan. It is also worth reviewing regularly.

Troubleshooting

Part of your customer service plan may include a trouble-shooting section. If you suspect that there is a percentage of business you lose because of a member of your team or problems with products, then having a follow-up plan to assess customer satisfaction is a great way to monitor what is going on.

Not all unhappy customers bother to complain to the right people and the loud and confused ones are potentially detrimental to your business if they tell their friends about their negative experience.

Some surveys suggest that as many as 90% of the customers you lose through perceived or real bad service will not even complain. They will just leave and not return. Making it easy for them to send you their comments, suggestions and feedback will make it easier for you to keep your finger on the pulse of your customer-service effectiveness.

It is much better to identify problem areas and empower your staff to sort these things out efficiently, thus keeping the focus on retaining the customer. This should also be the same when you get customer complaints of any kind. Develop a company policy of keeping the customer happy, even if you do lose the repeat business, so that he or she does not feel inclined to complain about lack of service, lousy meal, faulty products to anyone else but you.

Exceeding Your Customer's Expectations

This is part of your customer service plan – but you need to plan for it to happen. If you intend to send flowers or gifts when your customers have birthdays, or at Christmas time, then deciding to do this for your top 20%, or all of your customers, needs to be budgeted for. Splashing out by taking major clients to corporate events also needs to be budgeted for after you've thought through which events and/or gifts are most in keeping with your company and industry.

Announcing that you've scored a record-breaking contract or sale, making a big noise about it and 'casually throwing in a bonus' for the customer is something that needs to be decided ahead of time. Then your staff can be prepared to provide this 'freebie' in similar circumstances, even when you are not there. Using this sort of foresight means there's no risk of your happy customer crowing about his good fortune to someone else who may have topped the deal but missed out on the bonus – and who could be annoyed about not getting the same treatment.

As with all parts of your customer-service plan – decide ahead what your intentions are in various circumstances and set the wheels in motion ahead of time so those intentions become reality.

5

Increasing Market Share, Turnover and Profitability

Existing Customers

If you want to keep building up your business by getting a constant run of new customers to sell to or service, then you may be overlooking the importance of getting more out of your existing customers. In order to get exponential growth, you need to increase the number of customers, and increase the amount each customer spends and increase the profitability of each sale.

For example – let's say every average sale is $100; and you have 100 customers; and you expect a 30% margin on sales to give you a gross profit of $3000.

Increasing your customers to 105, each spending a new average of $105.00, and you increase your margins by an extra 5%, giving you a gross profit of $3858 – nearly a 30% increase.

Increasing your customers to 110, with a new spending average of $110, and leaving your margins at the new 5%

increase and you end up with an increase of gross profit of nearly 45%.

$ 100 Ave sale	$ 105 Ave sale	Just increasing 3,000 x 5% is: $3150.00. You get
X 100 Customers	X 105 Customers	exponential growth when you increase each part by
X 30%	X 31.5%	5% - which in this example is a nearly 16% increase
$3,000	$3472.87	overall.

However, it is very important to realize that just spreading the net wider does not always give you the return you want. Increasing the income you can get from many of your existing customers will not only be easier to achieve, as they are already familiar with your company, but with a good customer service plan in place, they will be happy to return to you and recommend others to you too.

You can also potentially raise your prices to reflect your superiority in the market, and encourage them to buy more from you more often. For most businesses, this is a highly recommended option for your marketing focus. First determine exactly what it is that reflects the real value you offer your customers – in their eyes. What *they* most appreciate about you, that they believe you can deliver better than your competitors, is what they are most willing to pay for. Once you are clear on this value proposition, enhance it and set your prices according to this, instead of being guided only by industry standard pricing.

6

Networking

Getting out and physically meeting new contacts is one of the best ways to grow your business. It's networking at its best when you can return from any function with at least half a dozen new contacts to follow up on. Using your audio logo is an important part of this process, and making the follow-up contacts and booking appointments is critical – otherwise you may as well stay home and watch TV.

Your local Chamber of Commerce, Rotary, Toastmasters, and various sporting clubs and associations offer a number of networking opportunities, and getting onto their invitation lists is as easy as calling to ask. Make a point of attending at least four networking events every year. Take a good supply of business cards, and pre-prepare your audio logo and follow-up lines (also called an 'elevator speech') ahead of time so they roll smoothly off your tongue.

In your marketing plan, identify the networking you will do to raise your profile in your targeted business community. Ensure you are formally networking in some way every month. This is the recommended minimum, and if you think you are too busy, consider just how critical this aspect of your marketing is.

"You also need to encourage others who work with or for you network, and to follow some simple networking guidelines so that this does become an effective part of your marketing strategy".

Six Basic Rules of Networking:
1. Do it regularly.
2. **Practice in advance**, what you are going to say when you introduce yourself or are asked about what you do.
3. **Use your Audio Logo** and Elevator Speech – *confidently.*
4. **Exchange business cards** with people you meet and *ask* if you may contact them for a meeting, and/or add them to your data-base so you can send them pertinent information.
5. **Follow up** potential leads within one week.

6. **Go back** out and repeat this process at least once every month.

From your networking, you will find people who may become clients, referrers, and centers of influence, as well as those who are ideal for prospecting.

Referrals & Centers of Influence

We all know people who love to tell other people about the new person they just met, or the thing they just bought. If you identify two or three of these wonderful walking advertisements for your business, nurture them and tell them why you are so happy to take them to lunch occasionally. Reward them generously for every referral they send to you.

These people are worth your time and appreciation. As part of your marketing plan, identify as many as five of these influential contacts and make them part of your networking and customer-services strategy. You can even make them feel involved in your business, by inviting them to become part of your team of mentors or advisors if this is appropriate.

In Malcolm Gladwell's international bestselling book, *The Tipping Point*, (published 2000, Little Brown and Company), he talks about influencers, mavens and connectors. These are the people who can have an enormous effect on your business. He also discusses how trends can turn to fads, and become blockbusters.

If you can identify the mavens, influencers and connectors within your range of network contacts, then I highly recommend getting this book and learning about this very special aspect of marketing.

Direct Prospecting

If targeted direct mail and prospecting is part of your plan, then you need refer back to part one, and identify what type of customers you serve, and what you can best do for them.

Setting up a specific *sales prospecting plan*, and tying it in with your *direct marketing plan* works best when your sales team is involved. Get them to sit the marketing team and yourself, to ensure that everyone's efforts complement each other.

Here's an easy way to prospect for new clients that is guaranteed to achieve much greater results than traditional cold calling using door knocking or telesales.

6 Steps to Successful Prospecting

1. Identify an *ideal client* you wish to work with – ensuring that the targeted company fits your best demographic and psychographic requirements.

2. Confirm the name of the top person you need to be in front of – the decision maker, not the junior staff.

3. Send them an attention-grabbing gift or promotional product including a letter stating your main reason

for contacting them, with a very basic outline of your skills in addressing challenges in their industry, and a promise to call within the next 48 hours.

4. Follow up with a phone call seeking 15 – 20 minutes of their time. Explain that you are aware of some of the frustrations experienced by companies when using your type of products or services, thus indicating that you are familiar with their needs.

5. Say that you would like to establish what their particular challenges are being quite positive that you will be able to offer improvements but that first you wish to make sure that there is in fact an opportunity to do business. In this way, you are demonstrating that, a) you can help and b) you're keen to save valuable time for both of you by doing your homework.

6. When you meet, be sure to take only 20 minutes of their time if that's what you agreed to. Be armed with prepared questions. Consider yourself to be on an information-gathering exercise and look for any chances where you can say, "If I can sort that out for you, can I come back to you with a proposal?" If the answer is yes – and why would it not be? – Then arrange to return within seven days.

Return and present the ways your company can help the prospective client meet whichever objective you have agreed on.

(For a scripted example of this process please see templates at the end of this book.)

It's very important to have your stationery, website, business cards and anything else that represents your company brand consistently matched and clearly identifiable. Messy or scruffy cards, or out of date contact details will be a potential turn off for your prospect.

Also be sure to have your email address fit with your company name, be easy to type in so as not to be accidentally ineffective, and to put a simple marketing message as a signature on your outgoing emails.

7

Branding = Projecting an Image

Your brand is not your logo, and your advertising is not your marketing. These are two common misconceptions that make 'marketing' quite complicated for some people. Terminology in many industries can trip up newcomers, but understanding these concepts can potentially save you thousands of dollars on advertising, marketing and branding.

Your Brand

This is everything that the customer experiences about you and your company. It includes the customer service, the look and feel of the service or products, interaction with staff, and what is seen and heard everywhere about you, right down to the way the man driving your company vehicle cuts others off at the traffic lights, or the noise and language made by the people hanging around outside your premises.

Branding is about image, and how the customer perceives your projection of 'who, what, why, where and when' you are; the *essence* of your company.

Your Logo

This is the badge or sign you use on your signage to indicate that 'this is where to find our brand of X'. It's like the arrow on the map, and the cherry on the pie. Logos need to be clearly identified and easy to see, so there is no mistaking yours for anyone else's in the crowd. Given that we are exposed to thousands of advertising images a day, yours needs to do its job: that is, to be distinctive.

Using simple lines, strong colors and above all else, consistency, in the representation of your logo is critical.

One thing to remember about logos is that some very good ones are not really logos at all. For example, consider the logo for 'HOLLYWOOD'... again, this is a recognized style using simple white letters and a consistent font.

You don't always have to have fancy pictures or graphics to call something a good logo.

Your Advertising

The short term message is *advertising* – long term messaging is marketing or brand building. Advertising is what you do when you tell someone what is happening in your business right now.

For example, *"there is a sale on"*, "we have new stock arriving daily", "we have won an award", and "the deal of the century is yours today". It may be that you use direct mail, flyers handed out on the street corner, or a range of media (both online or offline) to get this message out to your customers. There are many ways to do this and I encourage you to be specific in your approach to your target market, style of message or advertisement, copywriting and offer.

Brand Rules and Values

You need to make some firm ground rules for your business when you plan your marketing and how you will relate it to all of these areas such as Branding, Image, Logos, and Advertising.

Confirm your colors, style, fonts, use of logos and when or where you may allow deviation from your preferred use of these. For example, you may wish to use your logo mainly in the chosen company colors of red and blue, but at times you may need to default to a simple black and white, or gold or silver variation. Rules for covering the company rules in various situations should be decided in advance.

Decide on the type of advertising you wish to do; methods used to promote your company also needs to be consistent. Whether you choose radio, newspaper, direct mail, TV, Facebook, Google ads, or sandwich boards – your market will start to get familiar with your style of promotion, and become tuned in to it as long as you maintain consistency. Your brand values are those things that represent what you stand for. If you are selling tough-guy style clothing, and your target market is similar to that of 30+ year old males who like to drive SUV's and go fishing or hunting on weekends then some of your brand values may include durability, toughness, strength, and masculinity. If you are a high priced cosmetic company, then your brand values would more likely reflect things like softness, delicacy, luxury and expensiveness, or femininity.

Knowing your brand values helps to determine some of your branding rules. Our first example of tough-guy clothing would never be seen with fluffy pink fonts, or promoted by Boy George. Your rules would also state what kind of sponsorship or relative brand association your product or company would or would not entertain.

Everything is part of your branding, so you need to have rules for your branding and marketing that are well thought out, simple to follow and easy to understand. The customer service plan, advertising and media plan, and even your staff uniform plan are all part of your branding rules. It's like a Do's and Don'ts list of what you will and will not tolerate from within or for your organization.

Your Branding Rules

These are the rules of the company that you promote to your employees to use daily, and to ensure these are included in regular staff meetings and of course for everyone on Induction Day.

- There are fresh flowers at reception,
- Cars are clean and tidy,
- We look healthy and energetic,
- Our phones are answered promptly and with smiles,
- Our salespeople are positive,
- Our old uniforms are dumped – and no worn-out company branded T-shirts may be worn at the gym,
- Our logo is always accompanied by our positioning statement,
- Certain behaviors are noted regarding Social Media.

The list can be absolutely endless, but it is vitally important. So keep adding to it. Remember, every time your image is seen somewhere it (and your people) must be consistently representing your products, services and reinforcing the unique and special reasons why your company is better than its nearest competitor.

As soon as inconsistencies in your image show up they may make existing and potential customers feel a little unsettled about their relationship with you. Slowly the cracks may start to appear, leaving you vulnerable to a competitor's promotion.

Advertising and Media Plans

As stated in the last chapter, there is a difference between advertising and marketing, but you need to work out an annual media plan that charts proposed activities in both of these areas. This also helps to determine budgets and timing for everything.

One key mistake many advertisers make is to advertise with papers or radio stations they personally like to read or listen to. What you really need to do is identify what online and offline media options are best targeted to your market.

Which medium will give you the largest number of readers, listeners or viewers within your target, and the most effective cost per thousand? If you spend $1000 on one newspaper advertisement with a paper that boasts 10,000 readers, then your cost per thousand is $100, but if only 5000 of their readers are within your main demographic then really your cost per thousand is $200. If you run radio advertisements that give you 5000 pairs of ears within your targeted demographic, and the radio campaign costs $1000, then your cost per thousand is still $200.

(Take the cost of the advertisement and divide by number of listeners or readers to get cost per thousand).

If you only get 50 people responding to either of these advertisements, then you need to establish what the real cost of your campaign has been to get each prospect to respond.

CPT = $200, Cost per quantified lead = $20

If you are selling products that are only $50 each, then you would not call this a very successful campaign, but if each customer spends $5000, you might be quite happy with this response.

Here's an example of a media plan that is designed to help plan where you will advertise, and what you will spend each year in any or all of these areas.

Adding up each column and row gives you monthly totals and tells you how much you plan to spend on each option over the next 12 months. Working out this plan in advance each year helps you to stay focused on what your budget is and what you intend to change, or not, as different things arise.

Media Plan Example
Retail Gift Store

		Jan-March	Ap-Jun	Jul-Sep	Nov-Dec	Totals
Newspaper	Times	1500		1500		$ 3,000
Magazine	Better Home	2000	2000	2000	2000	$ 8,000
Radio	Classic Hits	2500		2500		$ 5,000
Directory	Regional	3200				$ 3,200
Sponsorship	Tennis Club		1000	1000		$ 2,000
Newsletters	Quarterly	1250	1250	1250	1250	$ 5,000
Online	FaceBook	1000	2000	2000	5000	$ 10,000
Promotion	Signage		3000		3000	$ 6,000
Biz Gifts	Pens	500		500		$ 1,000
Uniforms			1500			$ 1,500
	Totals	10450	10750	9250	11250	$ 44,700

Reach and Frequency

Let's expand the media plan further by breaking down the month of April into to May, when a promotion is scheduled and look at exactly what will be happening for 6 weeks before and after the promotion – promotion being a big sale during the weeks of the 22 – 29 Apri.

Media Plan Breakdown

Week Ending		15-Apr	22-Apr	29-Apr	6-May
Newspaper	1/4 page Sat	500	500	500	
Better Homes	Ads/Editorial		2000		
Radio Schedule	Drive time	750	750	750	
Newsletters	Database			1250	
Signs	Update Cars		1500		1500

This gives you a timeline of when things are going to happen and how it all fits together for this promotional sale, as well as the cost of each part of the advertising planned.

Online Advertising

It may well work for you to invest some of your budget into a range of online advertising options. The use of Facebook, Twitter, Instagram, Pinterest, and You Tube just to name a few has increased immeasurably in the last decade. However, the ability to implement good advertising and marketing on social media is fraught with issues for the uninitiated.

Whatever you decide to spend, how and where you place your online marketing budget, please be sure and work with a great SEO and online marketing specialist if you are not confident about doing this as a beginner.

Measuring the Results of your Advertising

Measuring the results you get from any investment in advertising is absolutely necessary. If you are not getting results, then change tactics. Otherwise you are simply making donations to someone.

Many businesses do not quantify their advertising costs by determining how many new enquiries come to them as a result of what they spend. You can test your results in several ways –

and the easiest is by asking people why they called, or came in to your store or office.

If you are stuck, then try one of these:

- *"How did you hear about us/our special?"*
- *"Would you mind telling me what prompted you to call us today?"*
- *"And how did you come to locate our number for this call?"*
- *"Have you heard any of our ads this week? Do you mind telling me which one(s)? What did you like about it/them?"*

Your customers and prospects won't mind answering such questions, and many of them may think even more highly of you when they know that you are constantly aiming at improving how you do things.

Using your website is another great way to track customers' reactions to your advertising and marketing messages. For example, coding a website address page with particular specials or information you are promoting, gives you the opportunity to see exactly what medium has been used to obtain this information. Try suggesting that there is a special offer for visiting your information site www.example.com/specials (example only) and then seeing how many people enter through that particular porthole.

You will be able to determine how often this has been used as an entry page with many web hosts, or you may like to track the peaks of your general visitor numbers and how they relate to your marketing activities.

Using Forms to Assess Turnover and Marketing Effectiveness

Here's an example of the type of simple form you could use for most types of small businesses to track your sales trends and conversion rates.

Number of Customers	Day	Number of Sales	Average $ Sale	Total Sales	Variables
12	M	5	60	300	Stormy all day
15	T	7	80	560	Still raining
20	W	11	57	623	
34	T	21	72	1512	1st day of sale
33	F	24	65	1560	
Total		=	=	=	Summary

You need to list your variables – for example, if it was raining, school holidays had started, there was a sale on, or a sale next door, a national holiday, a new salesperson... You can also add extra columns for things like, who was the salesperson, product or item category? At the end of each week, or whichever period of time you are assessing, you may start to see which days bring better business, which members of the team are out-performing the others, and what other variables are impacting on your turnover.

There are computer programs that make this sort of analysis easy but running even a simple manual version like this for a limited period of time is enough to give you useful information for assessment and planning purposes.

How did you hear about us?

A very simple form like this on the counter of your store or at the receptionist's desk is all you need to prompt yourself or staff to ask this simple question – how did you hear about us?

Media	✓	Total
TV		
Radio		
Newspaper		
Magazine		
Yellow pages		
Internet		
Existing customer		
Word of Mouth		
Passing by		
Billboards		
Other		

Working Out an Advertising Budget

Your advertising must be thought of as an investment – not an expense. Measure the results of what you do and if they are positive and increase your profits, then work out *where you are most comfortable* with increasing your investment. If you are a new business or trying a new method of advertising, consider how much you want to increase your sales or turnover by, and then take a small percentage of that increased turnover as your proposed trial budget.

For example, let's say you want to try advertising on the radio for the first time. You may want to increase your turnover by 20%, up from 500 to 600 units per week. Your products may have a $50 gross margin, affording you a *net profit increase* of $5000. So spending more than $5000 on a radio campaign to increase turnover by only 20% is false economy.

Here's an example of how to work out your advertising spend using these figures:

Product retails for $100 – Currently selling 5000 per week.

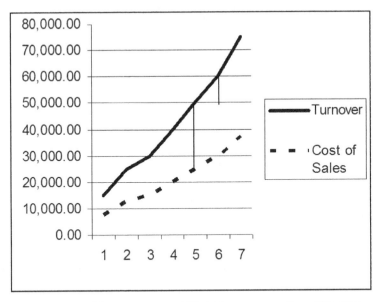

Total weekly turnover = $50,000, gross profit is $25,000

To increase sales by 20% above current turnover would increase turnover to $60,000, with a new gross profit of $30,000.

Therefore, in order to make the extra $5,000 gross profit, you may decide to spend up to, but not over, this amount.

Spending $2,000 to increase gross turnover by $10,000 per week may seem high, and it is possible to increase sales by spending a lot less on advertising. It is necessary to consider all of the variables in terms of longevity of the promotion, the natural run-on of increased turnover from this campaign and whether or not it is intended to raise capital, increase overall market share or quite excess stock.

Here's a simple formula next time you want to try something new:

Current average units sold	500	Units
X Gross profit /per unit	$50	GP per unit
X Targeted % Increase	20%	Targeted increase
= Increased turnover (GP)	$5000	Increased GP

If the medium you are considering testing is not going to possibly achieve any reach or frequency needed to make this work, then you need to consider what is possible with the budget you have to spend. Don't lose sight of the desired objective – increasing turnover of number of units sold by 20% (as per our example).

Some of your options may include direct mail letter to your top 30% of existing customers, or putting a small but very effective ad in the newspaper and having corresponding information on your website.

Consider your reason for advertising, test the options, and be confident that you have the right product, and the price is right for the market you are targeting.

Getting Your Advertising to Work

If your advertising doesn't work, first assess the copy – was the headline or style of advertisement designed to hit the market you are aiming at? Then determine if the offer was a good one. You may need to ask some of your customers what they thought of it to really know the answer to this question. Was the advertisement featured often enough and prominently enough to reach the target market?

If all of these pan out, then check to see how many enquiries you had, and what the sales conversion rate was. A general rule of thumb in the advertising industry suggests that so long as the copy, offer and reach and frequency were good, then the problem more than likely lies in the ability of the sales people to secure the orders.

Don't advertise just for the sake of being seen to be waving the flag. This is no better than making a donation to the media. Your short term advertising must have a call to action. A 'something' that tells people when, why or how to do what you want them to do.

Just saying *'we're here, come spend your money at our place'* is only effective if you intend to do this over a long period of time. This is marketing, and needs to be consistent and measured by long term peaks and troughs, not short term fluctuations in store traffic.

Also, it's important to test different headlines. One or two words can sometimes make the difference between everyone wanting your products and no one being interested at all.

For example, if you are advertising something like a sale on suits, there are three ways to say the same thing – but consider the impact of each different headline on the potential outcomes.

Suits for sale

--oOo--

50% off new suits this week only

--oOo--

Impress the boss and save up to $500

8

Promotions

The following is a good checklist for both advertisements and promotions in a more general sense.

The four key ingredients to ensuring success of a promotion:

1. **The right target market** – knowing your demographics and psychographics of your ideal target market and how best to reach them

2. **The right message** – knowing that your target market is most likely to want to know about your particular message, promotion or event

3. **The right timing** – ensuring that your promotion is happening at the best time – for example, not having a special offer on air conditioners in the middle of winter or heaters in summer

4. **Getting their attention** – making sure that your target market is aware of what you are promoting

As we've already covered target markets extensively, let's discuss the last three.

The right message tells your target market that you are doing something of interest to them. For example... if your target is teenagers and you are having a sale of stylish HOLDEN brand clothing that they are into, they will want to know about your sale. If you are selling brand-new HOLDEN Commodore cars, there is a strong likelihood that only a very small percentage of teenagers will be able to afford them, and so promoting to them won't work.

If you are selling HOLDEN brand clothing and giving away tickets to BATHURST, some teenagers will want to know about it, but more of their fathers may be responsive to the promotion.

Getting the timing right means thinking through the realities of why people buy things when they do. Offer a house spring-cleaning service in midwinter and the response rate is bound to be lower than the same offer made later, in spring, when more homeowners are thinking about getting ready for selling their homes or entertaining in them.

Getting their attention requires planning, forethought, and smart decision-making about how best to reach them with your message at the right time. You can use a range of options, including electronic or print media, signs, direct mail or even dragging people off the street into your store, if that is what it takes! Let's explore some of the more popular options.

9

Media Options

There are many ways to promote yourself and 'multi-media' ATL, or BTL (above or below the line advertising) may be a term you'll hear a lot as you navigate your own marketing minefield. Let's explore the main ones: radio, TV, newspaper, magazines, billboards, internet, and promotional products.

Print Media
Newspapers

For example, a newspaper advertisement with potential to reach 150,000 readers (of whom, only 1500 may actually be prospects for your products and services), may require two to five ads, at a cost of $500 to $5000 per advert.

We know that targeted readers will most likely need to be exposed to your message more than once before they will be ready to respond. But newspapers tend to be read either in the morning, or evening, but not traditionally at a time that will result in an immediate response.

In addition, today's newspaper is tomorrow's birdcage liner, so the window of opportunity for response is very short.

Magazines

These are generally read when first purchased, although some may linger for a while. Regardless of whether they are weekly, monthly, or quarterly, a typical magazine normally lasts only as long as it takes to be replaced by the next issue.

Magazines are often more specifically targeted than other media, offering advertising that appeals directly to the market that buys or subscribes to it. For time-sensitive promotions, you can target generally, although you never know when (or if) the magazine will actually be read. In addition, magazine advertising is often sold based on the number of copies printed, rather than sell-through figures. It not always well known that that many of the magazines appearing in bookstores and other retail outlets never sell out before the next issue arrives. In those cases, the front covers are torn off and returned to the publisher for credit, while the rest of the issue, including all those great ads, are thrown away by the store owner.

Magazine salespeople use both circulation data and readership data to convince people to buy. Circulation data is based on officially audited numbers of copies sold; 'readership' is a measure of how many people have seen, glanced through or read a magazine recently (a much higher figure as it includes people who casually pick them up at dentists, takeaways, airlines lounges and friends' homes) Advertisers should ask which set of figures salespeople are spouting to them. Magazine readership surveying is going on all the time and certainly indicates trends which the media industry relies on. Small-circulation, specialist magazines are exempt from this entire official tracking however, so are much harder to get reliable info about.

Electronic Media
Radio

Radio is more likely to be heard regularly through the day, perhaps at times more conducive to getting people to respond to your message. Radio is instant. It used to be and in many cases it still is, that if something is happening (whether locally or internationally) you are very likely to hear about it on the radio. If you hear a rumour, you may listen to the news at the top of the hour to check out the story. In this way, radio is a recognized source of news and information. We also go online for a lot of our news now and search the internet for updates on any event unfolding, but that does not mean that people still don't turn on their TVs or Radios for the 'formal reports'.

For radio to be effective, you must ensure that your message is simple, has impact, and is heard *often enough* to reach your targeted market. By often enough, I mean at least three times a day. To ensure that happens, you may need to schedule at least five to eight advertisements per day (depending on timing), to allow for the times that listeners are busy or away from their radio.

Essentially, this means that a successful radio campaign may need as many as ten commercials per day over several days or weeks to be truly effective, at a cost of hundreds or even thousands of dollars per day, depending upon the size of your market. And while a radio station may offer you access to 100,000 listeners, it's possible that only a few dozen are good prospects for what you have to offer. This is particularly true of business-to-business marketers who offer a highly specialized product.

For example, how many people listening to the radio in any given day have the need for a high-quality camera? Perhaps some, but will it be enough to justify the cost of reaching tens of thousands of non-prospects as well?

Both radio and newspaper are essentially short-term advertising options that must have an immediate effect, and be run continuously in order to generate consistent results.

Television

Television advertising can be very effective, but it costs quite a lot to create and schedule an effective television ad. If it is part of your marketing plan, and you can maintain the high cost of production and repeated airings, then it may be worthwhile. However, even in this case, supporting television with at least one other form of advertising is recommended.

Television viewers often "tune out" either physically or mentally during commercials. They do this by channel surfing, talking, leaving the room or even editing out ads when recording a favorite program. For this reason, broadcasters are increasingly beginning to offer "product placements," a subtle type of advertising, which includes a company's logo or product as part of the action within the program itself.

Big companies like Pepsi and McDonalds are able to do this as a way to increase brand awareness – but it is far too expensive to be a practical option for local car dealers, banks or furniture retailers.

Note – long-term radio and television program sponsorship can be a good brand-building option for marketers, but cost is high and responsiveness is almost impossible to measure.

Billboards

A billboard will typically appear for several weeks, and your message will be exposed to a high number of motorists driving by. But while billboards are helpful with branding, they are generally not very successful at getting an instant response to your message (unless the message happens to contain the words, "Exit Here!").

Some companies have used billboards very successfully to drive the awareness of their brand in recent years, and billboard marketing has increased as a regular option for many marketers. Some of the most talked about billboard campaigns in New Zealand was the 'Yeah Right' series run by the Tui Beer company, which was then copied by another leading beer brand in New Zealand. Market share for both brands has increased dramatically over the past few years. Bendon also successfully used non-conservative imaging on billboards to help revolutionize the lingerie industry in the 1990's. And of course when you draw near to any airport in the land you'll see an abundance of billboards promoting everything from phone services, to duty free stores, airlines, and luxury items.

These examples all used multi-media campaigns, however their billboards are widely recognized and talked about adding to the high visibility of their brands.

In some countries, you can see a lot of mobile billboards in the form of buses, cars and trucks that have significant signage applied to their exteriors. They can be a great way of brand building, but consider the target market that you are aiming for. Some products may be better suited to this than others.

Yellow Pages and Directories

Directories such as the Yellow Pages may be a valuable tool if your buyers have already decided they are in the market for your product or service. In this type of advertising, it is important to tell the buyer who you are, and why they should call *you* before they call any of the sixteen or so other similar companies that may be advertising on the same page.

With the increased use of web marketing, and the ability to directly link your online yellow pages advertisement to your own website, there are now many options to consider with this medium. However, you can update your print advertisement in the Yellow Pages book only once a year. As a result, special promotions are out, as are any other time-sensitive events. And while the yellow pages and many other online directories can sound like a good deal, remember to check the statistics for your business on how many people are simply 'Googling' to find your business or someone who can provide your products or services. You may well find that increasing your online marketing strategy more than makes up for decreasing your directory advertising.

Direct Mail

As an advertiser, you want the best possible response from the maximum number of clients to achieve the most cost effective outcome for your money. In the past, direct mail was considered a hit-and-miss option.

Traditional direct mail provided a 1 to 3% response rate *if you were lucky*, and therefore could be very expensive and wasteful. However, smarter technology has led to more effective forms of direct marketing, which can be improved even more dramatically with the use of promotional products.

Personalized direct mail sent to previous and current contacts reaches people who already know who you are. As a result, they are much more likely to be receptive to your marketing. This can include anyone you've had dealings with in the past six months (such as suppliers, contractors, unsuccessful quote recipients, etc.) And while your direct mail might cost an average of $2.00 for each letter (including a small gift such as a refrigerator magnet), you will have a much better chance of striking the right note with existing contacts.

Including a promotional item that will be *kept longer than the letter itself* increases your branding exposure and your likelihood of success, even when using a mailing list not made up of existing contacts.

If the recipient doesn't react to your advertisement or offer immediately, they will still likely keep the gift (with your name and marketing message on it), which keeps you in front of them and positions you to make a sale when they are ready to purchase.

Many studies have determined that sending a personal letter directly to your target market, with a promotional product, will increase the effectiveness of your direct mail campaign. Try it with your next mailing and test the results. You will very likely see an increase in readership and response over sending out a mailing piece alone.

Promotional Products

This makes up a very large part of the marketing industry worldwide, and refers to any item with a logo used to promote a brand or industry. This includes T-shirts, caps and various clothing items; office accessories such as calendars and diaries, sticky notes and pens; watches and electronic equipment; computer accessories such as mouse pads and memory sticks; bags and sports items; toys, novelties and gadgets, and house wares.

It is estimated that there are more than 600,000 different types of promotional products, and it's constantly changing.

If you are considering using promotional products as either thank-you gifts, a gift with purchase, or to get someone's attention, then talk with a good promotional product professional who understands that business and can work with you on achieving the best outcomes. There is a lot more to it than simply putting a logo on a mug or T-shirt, and some outstanding results can be had by working with an expert in this area.

Online Media

Getting the right social media marketing mix, with a combination of Google Adwords, Facebook, You Tube, Twitter, Instagram, Pinterest, or Linked In advertising is something that will work incredibly well if you also have excellent SEO (Search engine optimization) to support your SEM (Search engine marketing). You also need an excellent, functional, and well optimized website to support your business and online marketing strategy too. While this is an expected area for many advertising budgets to focus on, this is just about a whole book on its own. And there are many great ones out there. My best recommendation is to learn all you can about this, and then engage some well experienced experts for their help in getting started with online marketing strategies to support all your offline branding, marketing and advertising efforts.

There are multiple ways to achieve excellent outcomes with online marketing. Getting your own keywords well promoted and embedded into your content takes strategy, expertise, and I highly recommend you work with someone who really does know what they are doing in this area before you go off and spend a lot of money.

Not only do the rules change quite regularly, but those who do specialize in this form of ATL marketing need to keep abreast of the trends, changes, and to know where to predictably put your money so that you can get a good return.

10

Building a Strong Reputation

You don't have to rely on spending money on advertising to get people wanting to do business with you. You also don't have to have enormous budgets to get great media coverage for your business. One of the best ways to become known for something is to get someone to write about you and get it published.

News Releases and Public Relations

Making sure that people know who you are can come from simply being newsworthy and interesting, and making sure the story you have to tell is passed on to the media properly.

Regardless of what your industry or business is about, when you release a new service, product, win an award, or achieve something that may be interesting for people in your community, business network or trade, it's important to get a good news release out to the relevant media and tell people about it.

This costs you nothing more than the preparation of the news release and some time to distribute it and follow up if necessary.

The best part about doing this is the media usually appreciates information that has a good newsworthy angle, especially when they don't have to go looking for it in dark corners. Shine a light on yourself and what you are doing, and see what happens.

The other great part about this form of marketing is that most of what we read in the papers or hear on the news is considered to be far more credible than the same information we might see or hear as an advertisement. This is because we usually associate *news* items with being factual (outside of tabloid news items), and therefore we tend to believe it more readily.

Preparing a Good News Release

These are ideally only one page long and will state your news or information succinctly and in a newsworthy way. A new-product launch is newsworthy, for instance, especially if it can be seen to be beneficial to some section of the community.

Winning an award takes on a new shine if you can add that there was a stiff entry process, that significant challenges were overcome, or that your company will benefit from this new product, award or contract and that this means new jobs in your area. You have to make it interesting and relevant to the readers.

Think about how your news will affect people and write it that way.

Always include your contact details for any editors who may wish to obtain further information or an interview.

Develop a media list that includes the most effective outlets for your company's news and information. Include national and local newspapers, radio newsrooms, magazines, and trade and business publications and TV if you think it's appropriate. Of course you also need to consider adding in online news and blog sites that are relevant and will run a story about you.

Many editors are now happy to receive releases as emails (copy the press release into the main body of the email; don't send it as an attachment), but it may pay to check your intended editor's preferences.

Follow up a day or two after you send your press release. Don't ask 'did you get my press release'. Instead offer to be available for any further information or interviews, and assume that they did receive it.

Hire a publicist if you think you need professional help with your public relations.

Networking, Writing and Speaking

There are lots of ways to get out and meet people who will send you referrals or come to you for your services. Getting to know people can be very intimidating for many of us, but don't forget that just about everyone you meet at a networking event is suffering from the same problem... they all want to meet other people but are a little shy of talking to complete strangers.

Try finding someone in the room who looks uncomfortable or is standing alone and introduce yourself. Guaranteed, they will most likely hang on to you like a limpet for a few minutes, out of sheer joy at being saved from drowning in a sea of networkers who all have someone else to talk to already.

Push yourself to be socially pro-active like this and it won't take long to glean several new contacts who will think you are great (for rescuing them). You'll be seen as popular and others will want to talk to you too. This is the best way I know to make networking really easy if you are new to it.

The rewards are excellent, due to the increased exposure you will get for your business, and the new contacts who will hopefully promote you to their associates.

Stand up and Shout

Speaking at trade events, conferences, and networking meetings is another excellent way of building on your credibility as an expert in your chosen field. Seeking out these opportunities is a great way to shine the spotlight on your business.

If you are shy of talking to groups you can learn to overcome this by joining Toastmasters. Some of the greatest speaking professionals and many award-winning orators started out unable to put two words together in front of a crowd of three people before joining Toastmasters. If this doesn't work for you, then another option is to identify someone else in your company to be your spokesperson or public representative.

One other option is to hire a celebrity to take on this role for you. However, this could be a very expensive option, and the celebrity would need to understand your business very well in order to effectively represent you.

A few years ago I was consulting to a large garden supply company in New Zealand. A talented young landscape designer was just starting to be seen on national television gardening shows as a support person to the main star, and the company really liked the look of her. I approached her directly and asked if she'd be interested in meeting my clients. She agreed to drive two hours south for a meeting over lunch, which ultimately resulted in her being supported to further advance her dreams of becoming a celebrity landscape gardener while at the same time her celebrity status was linked to their company in many positive ways.

It doesn't always have to be a big (expensive) star for there to be a mutually beneficial outcome when approaching the idea of having a recognizable voice for your company.

Write About It

We all have a valued talent in something. Deciding to extend that talent into absolute expertise means learning everything you can about it and then finding a way to share that expertise with others. It will increase your value to your customers significantly and highlight your business to your readers.

If you are not comfortable writing your own material, you can hire good writers to do this for you.

There are numerous ways you can use your writing to grow your business. Newsletters can go out to your clients and prospect list several times each year. A regular column in your local paper or a trade magazine that reaches your target market will also help to profile you as an expert in your field.

Writing a regular blog that can even be turned into a collection of articles and ultimately a book is also an excellent way to become a recognized author-ity in your field.

11

Websites and Social Media Marketing Tools

Before you start investing in a great website, you need to consider its function as a marketing tool for your business. There are thousands of cute, pretty, interesting, and dramatically different websites in the internet, but many of them are simply 'so what' in terms of contributing to people's perception of what a business is about. A great design and lots of flashy moving pictures will not hook a potential customer unless there is a strong incentive to go beyond the home page and delve a little deeper.

Annoying mobile shapes or words that dance across the page will turn most people off and send them searching for your competitors. Anything that takes more than a moment to download, scan (not necessarily read) is a waste of time. The faster we become at seeking and finding information, the more spoilt we become. Today's demand is for speed and simplicity. Consumers have become so effective at deleting unnecessary clutter and homing in on the information they want that speed and efficiency rule, while 'superfluous hype' withers on the sidelines.

As part of your marketing tool kit, at the very least your website must have the following:

'Home' page – like the cover of a good book, it must have enough information to draw the visitor in, be welcoming, clean, and clearly understood at a glance. It must also be consistently branded and easily recognizable as being part of your business. The logos and colors need to match what visitors are already familiar with from other marketing tools you use, such as business card, signs, premises, and people.

'Contact Details' page – this should be as simple as a touch of a button to email a request for more information, or if you must gather details about who is contacting you, don't make it long and arduous. Keep it brief – with a comments section that the visitor may use to explain his or her enquiry a little more. Asking for name, address, phone number, industry type, birthday, zip codes at this point makes most people wary of being harvested for a database that will start generating unwanted spam.

Ideally, your contact page should also have a postal address and phone number. After all, picking up the phone and talking to a real person is far more preferable for many people – even in this age of texting and digital imagery.

Always include international phone and zip codes for your business – you never know who may want to reach you, and remember that the internet *is* global.

An 'About Us' page – tell the visitor a little about who and what you are about. The type of services or products you provide, and the type of customers you may work with.

From there you may wish to go into more details about your products, services, history, and even provide testimonials from happy customers – but remember to keep it simple and not to oversell. If you want people to talk with you about how you can best serve them, make it easy and inviting for them to contact you for more information. Don't give it all away on the website by answering all their questions – leave the door open for genuine enquiry to come to you so that you can sell to them.

Your website is a more powerful tool than a brochure or advertisement, because you can make it interactive and provide a wider range of information, but using it to do all the work of opening, closing, and banking the sale makes you lazy and prevents interaction that many people still want.

If your business is supposed to be selling items directly from your website, then use a shopping-cart feature that makes purchasing easy, straightforward (ask yourself whether a ten year old could easily work through your online ordering forms) and secure. Post a guarantee on your site to ensure that people are confident that they can contact you and get their money back if they are genuinely unhappy with their purchase.

Regularly check that your shopping cart function is working *exactly* as it should.

There is major frustration born of not being able to complete a purchase online simply because something has changed (for whatever reason) and won't accept input of a required field.

Remember, whatever frustrates and irritates someone is likely to turn them off and nudge them towards someone else's business (your competitor?) both in real stores and cyber business sites.

What is Social Media?

Facebook, Linked In, Twitter, Blogging, You Tube – these are arguably still the most popular online marketing tools in the Social Media toolbox. There are many others but for most business operators right now, these are the core essentials to launching your social media services.

Collectively, they provide a platform of up-to-date information about your business activities – special offers, reviews and news. Media tools provide your business with ways to communicate with your customers, developing loyalty and repeat business.

Is Social Media Necessary?

Absolutely! With the world at their fingertips, customers can switch from your business to your competitor's in a heartbeat. Integrating social media initiatives with your marketing plans is critical to establishing and maintaining your market presence. When your website and social media is working well, you have direct access to your customers at all times – a powerful marketing advantage for any business!

My recommendation for anyone wanting to master their social media platforms and develop workable websites and online marketing strategy is to talk with someone who really knows what they are doing in this area. There are countless experts out there.

Knowing who you can trust starts with looking at what they are already doing, achieving, and their reputation with other specialists in the online marketing industry. Don't be afraid to ask a lot of questions, and expect to see them walking their talk with their own websites and social media platform management.

12

Planning is the Key to

Your Marketing Success

No matter how well you understand the principles and ideas outlined in this book, if you don't plan your use of them in the form of a media and marketing plan, then you are likely to lose money and response potential.

If you take some time to ensure that you have integrated your marketing properly so that all the pieces fit together and your branding works with your advertising and your customer services complement your marketing strategy, then your message is likely to be much more clearly received by your target market.

You also need to ensure that your planning leads to a well-orchestrated marketing effort. Imagine an orchestra lined up and ready to play but bereft of a conductor there to keep everyone in time together. Instead of beautiful music, you would end up with chaos and noise; so too with your marketing. Someone needs to lead the way and keep it all flowing smoothly.

Finally, it is critical that your marketing efforts are clearly targeted to the most lucrative target market – in other words, pick the lowest hanging fruit. Who will spend the most, more readily, and become a raving fan of your business, product or service? That's who you want to direct most of your marketing towards securing as your customers.

And of course – don't forget that marketing can be fun – so enjoy being creative, but don't blind your clients and prospective customers by being too flashy, or deafen them by being too loud, unless you really are a circus!

Summary

This is about putting it all together. Targeting the right mix of potential customers, getting the timing right and offering something that will get everyone knocking your doors down to get what you are offering.

Remembering the following formula will help to keep it all together. The three points to remember all this are:

Targeted Marketing

You need the right demographic and psychographic prospective customer mix. To clearly articulate the exact people you are aiming for – to know clearly who makes the most ideal type of customer for you will reduce the costs of marketing to them, and increase your marketing effectiveness. You should be assured of reaching the most people who will spend the most money on your particular service or product, with the least amount of overall effort on your part.

Orchestrated

Get the timing right – just as a conductor keeps the orchestra in time with each section and creates beautiful music using a variety of instruments and sounds, someone needs to be in charge of the whole marketing program so that all the media and all of the various branding elements work together.

Integrated

All of the marketing you do must be tied together, the branding materials must be consistent, and the media and advertising needs to fit with each other.

In conjunction with the basics of **Who** your customers are, **What** you really do for them, and **Why** they are buying from you instead of your competitors, Extreme Marketing works as part of keeping your planning and your WHOLE marketing focus all easy to follow and implement – not just once or twice, but all year, every year.

In order to be truly effective, your promotions and your advertising messages need to be:
- Targeted to the right mix of people,
- Timed to reach them at the best time,
- Delivering the right message or offer,
- Attention grabbing.

Your marketing requires regular scheduled promotions and advertising, with public relations support such as newsworthy press coverage, editorial features and a strong brand plan.

TEMPLATES AND FORMS

The following pages are the repeated forms and guidelines used throughout this book that you may like to use, adapt, print and give to your staff as required.

As purchaser of this book you are entitled to use them as you like, however under copyright law, you may not re-sell them, use them in public training sessions or use them for any other commercial purposes without the permission of the publishers.

Targeted Prospecting
for New Business

Step 1 – Identify the companies you wish to be working with.

Step 2 – Find out the name of the person you wish to meet with and discuss the opportunities – make sure he/she is a KEY DECISION MAKER

Step 3 – Send a prospecting letter – with an attention seeking package

Step 4 – Follow up the letter with a phone call in 3-4 days. Your objective – to get a meeting with the decision maker – that's ALL!!!

Step 5 – Meet the decision maker – take only 20 minutes to discuss what they are unhappy or frustrated about e.g. the current electrical contractor and/or need they may have for expanding into using a new/extra contractor

Step 6 – Arrange to send them a formal proposal or outline of what your company can do for them – in the next few days.

Step 7 – Follow up with phone call or hand deliver that proposal and get the business!!!

Prospecting Direct Letter – Template

Letter goes with a stress ball or similar suitable business toy...

<Electrician/ contractor/plumber/builder>
<Recipient Address Details>

Hello <PROSPECT *first name*>

Imagine the scene – Your regular <tradesperson> is a one-man-operation who sadly takes ill unexpectedly. Then when you **finally** locate an <tradesperson> who specializes in ...., you discover that it may take up to 3 weeks (longer at some times of the year) to get him or her to turn up. That certainly adds to the stress levels and can cost you more than just lost time!

We understand this kind of stress and job cost very well, and would like to assure you of two key ingredients when you enlist the services of one of our team:

We don't work alone, we have a team of qualified tradespeople available to work on a variety of projects, so you can be assured we will be on hand whenever you need us.

We are able to work more efficiently than most in our industry due to the superior systems we have in place –

What this means to you is that we are available, we're great on the job and on the paperwork, and our staff are the best in the business – guaranteed!

We'd like to meet with you briefly and introduce you to our special (and some say unique) way of operating, and determine just how many ways we can be of great service to your company. You can be sure of one thing – knowing just what makes us so special is time well spent – if not now, certainly it will pay off for you in the future.

I'll call you in the next few days to arrange to spend 15 – 20 minutes with you that we're sure will impress you – and that's even before you experience our outstanding on-the-job excellence!

Kind Regards,

Scripted Follow Up:

YOU: Hello May I speak with <...> please?

Hi   <...>, this is <Name> from <Business) in <town or city name> calling to follow up with you about a letter we sent to you this/last week. You may recall this was in relation to <Name of Business> special services that we'd love for your company to be aware of.

(Your primary objective in this call is to get the appointment – to get face to face (or if using Skype or Zoom), a live meeting - do not try to do the sale of your services or product over the phone.

How many of your competitors in the trades would go to this sort of trouble to get a face-to-face meeting with a prospect? This system works!!!!

This might even seem a little old fashioned, given that a lot of people think that just sending email marketing letters is easy, but more targeted and personal approaches still work incredibly well because they are targeted, personal, and not a lot of people bother to do this stuff anymore. If you want to stand out – the Zig while others are Zagging!

Follow Up Meeting

Objectives for the meeting held with prospective new client

1)   Identify if there are **any problems** prospect has had with your competitors in the past?

2)   What are the **primary requirements** of that prospect in relation to their current situation with your competitor(s)?

3)   Ask about their **unique** and **special** needs?

4)   Ask if there is any potential for your company to return with a more personalized presentation or option for your companies to begin working together? - If so, then go through the same DAY/TIME/PLACE scenario as you did with obtaining the first meeting, and don't leave until you have a definite arrangement for you to return with a customized quotation or proposal.

5)   Leave the prospect with an information pack.

6)   Return a few days later – as arranged – to outline specifically how your company can benefit this prospect, and what the details of that arrangement would entail.

If the prospect sees value in this proposal, get him/her to sign the 'accept the quotation/proposal/ form, and then file it with your office. Prospect has become a client, and you should already have all his/her contact and quotation details in the proposal.

Follow up this meeting with a brief letter thanking him/her for their time, enclosing a small gift (desk object with your logo and contact details), and assuring him/her of your best attention at all times. Also check that he/she has an extra copy of your business card and the names and contact details of any additional members of your team that they may need.

About Dixie Maria Carlton

A successful author, publisher, international speaker and coach, Dixie has taken dozens of authors and business specialists **from Idea to Author-ity®.**

Based in Brisbane Australia, but well-travelled, Dixie has worked with clients all over the world, from a variety of industries. Dixie's special skills combining all her experience in marketing, brand development, publishing, speaking and coaching make up her essential toolbox when working with highly motivated entrepreneurs who want to change their corner of the world.

Dixie's own mission is to help bring their important messages that matter to their target market. Exceptional at strategy, able to clearly see the big picture and understand the details. She is described by clients as methodical, knowledgeable and inspirational.

To request more information on how you can work with Dixie, or have her speak at your next event, please email: Dixie@dixiecarlton.com

Other books by Dixie Maria Carlton

- The Taboo Conversations/That Sex Book
- From Idea to Author-ity
- Golden Nuggets – for young people who grow up and go

Collaborative books featuring Maria Carlton
- The Power of Promotional Products
- The Power of More Than One
- The Power of More Than One – v2
- 20/20 – A Fresh Look at Business Growth
- 20/20 – A Fresh Look at Inspiration
- Create the Business Breakthrough You Want

Dixie also writes Fiction as Dixie Carlton
- A Song Out of Time – Part 1 of the Margaret McKenzie Story
- Rhythm and Rhyme – Part 2 of the Margaret McKenzie Story
- Beyond the Shadows
- Hell Hath No Fury
- The Choices Series – due for release 2019

You can access Dixie Maria Carlton's Author Page via this link:
www.tinyurl.com/DMCarlton

www.dixiecarlton.com
Facebook.com/dixiecarltonauthor

Twitter.com/dixiecarlton
Instagram.com/curatingconversations

Made in the USA
Middletown, DE
08 January 2019